Table of Contents

A Salubrious Steampunk Welcome - 6

A Treatise on the Use of This Oracle for Divination, Contemplation and Inspiration - 11

The Laying Down of Cards - 18

One-Minute Messages - 128

About the Author - 139

About the Artist - 141

CARD STORIES

1. Galago - 28
2. Carpenter Bee - 30
3. Anglerfish - 33
4. Praying Mantis - 35
5. Meerkat - 38
6. Nautilus - 40
7. House Wren - 43
8. Dragonfly - 45
9. Puffer Fish - 47
10. Wombat - 50

MAXINE GADD'S
Zoologica
THE STEAMPUNK ORACLE

LEELA J. WILLIAMS

MAXINE GADD'S
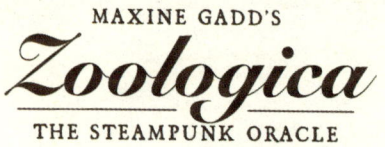
THE STEAMPUNK ORACLE

Copyright © 2024 Leela J. Williams
Artwork © 2024 Maxine Gadd

All rights reserved. Other than for personal use, no part of these cards or this book may be reproduced in any way, in whole or in part, without the written consent of the copyright holder or publisher. This publication is intended for spiritual and emotional guidance only. The content is not intended to replace medical assistance or treatment. The views and opinions expressed by the author, both within and outside of this publication, do not necessarily reflect the views of the publisher.

Published by Blue Angel Publishing®
80 Glen Tower Drive, Glen Waverley, Victoria, Australia 3150

info@blueangelonline.com
www.blueangelonline.com

Edited by Peter Loupelis and Cherise Asmah
Designed by Sunshine Connelly
Blue Angel Publishing® is a registered trademark of Blue Angel Gallery Pty. Ltd.

ISBN: 978-1-922573-97-1

11. Cicada - 53
12. Chameleon - 55
13. Sea Jellies - 57
14. Little Brown Bat - 59
15. House Fly - 62
16. Tortoise - 64
17. Koala - 66
18. Spanner Crab - 69
19. Tree Frog - 72
20. Nine-Banded Armadillo - 74
21. Spider - 76
22. Bilby - 78
23. Humboldt Squid - 81
24. Hermit Crab - 84
25. Scarab Beetle - 87
26. Dumbo Octopus - 90
27. Long-Eared Owl - 92
28. Clawed Lobster - 94
29. Butterfly - 96
30. Pangolin - 99
31. Stone Crab - 102
32. Giant Isopod - 105
33. Seahorse - 107
34. Garden Snail - 109
35. Axolotl - 113
36. Long-Horned Beetle - 115
37. Oranda Goldfish - 117
38. Horseshoe Crab - 121
39. Shoebill Stork - 123
40. Boxfish - 125

A SALUBRIOUS STEAMPUNK WELCOME

The ingenious beings of *Maxine Gadd's Zoologica* exist in a changed world that connects past and future, history and fantasy. Most are self-engineered, inspired by creatures who live in parallel zones or face comparable challenges. Others, like Koala and Meerkat, experienced powerful adaptations of consciousness whereby they now employ tools and mechanisms from the human world to navigate their altered reality. They are all resourceful, resilient and innovative. I am so very grateful to Maxine for inviting me into their space and trusting me to be the conduit for their messages.

Sitting with these creatures and delving into their tales has been an extraordinary process. They led me into realms dark and bizarre, curious and playful. They revealed treasure, alchemy and unusual truths. Underlying all the tales was the triumphant fact that these beings are intelligent and intentional adapters. Shifting sands, dissolving horizons and confounding discombobulation have been met with graceful strategy, experimental tinkering and unflappable discipline. They looked forward and became their future selves.

Wrapping words around the wisdom of this strange menagerie was a daunting task. The insight journey was anachronistic, fantastical, imaginative, unfamiliar and utterly marvellous. It was well beyond my humble reach, so I turned to mentors who knew this territory. You may recognise shades of H.G. Wells, Mary Shelley, Jules Verne, Lewis Carroll, Edgar Allan Poe, Neil Gaiman, Terry Pratchett, Arthur Conan Doyle, G.K. Chesterton and other writers who influenced the steampunk movement.

With the help of these esteemed character creators and world builders, I figured I'd aim for the stars, and even when I fell short and missed the moon, I'd come crashing and burning into a volcanic gateway to the centre of the earth, plummet leagues beneath the sea or catch a ride on a marvellous machine. Whatever happened, it would be a grand adventure – and it was!

In fitting with the steampunk genre, these remarkable creatures and inventions have some strange tales to tell and quirky ways of expressing themselves. Some are complex and cryptic, others poetic and allusive. Welcome the unfamiliar and ambiguous as part of your oracular process.

Socrates, whose philosophical influence stretches from ancient Greece to modern times, didn't write anything down. He saw the written word as inferior to dialogue that could be adapted to suit the situation and audience. Ideas that become fixed on paper, are fluid in spoken exchange and continue to evolve. Adaptability, innovation and evolution are common threads for steampunk and Socrates. The Zoologica have coined a word to describe their collection of stories: *idio-Socratic*. They are peculiar, individual, indefinable, adaptable, innovative and ever evolving.

I once took a class at university called *A History of Magic*. One lecture began with the challenge of deciphering a blurry image. We were to write down what we saw. Our lecturer then showed a second slide of the same image but a little more in focus. Again, we were to write about what we saw. This continued until the picture was in sharp focus. Many of us had intuited the image on the second or third slide and then elaborated on the detail with each slide. We were feeling pretty good about our slightly-above-average powers of deduction.

And then, our lecturer explained that when the same exercise was done with shamans or seers from various areas, they offered utterly different stories for each slide. Even when the image shown was completely crisp, what they described might have nothing to do with the literal picture. This reminded me of many of the mediums and intuitives I've known over the years, as well as my own experience with tarot where a card can have a new story to tell in every reading.

Divination tools, be they crystal balls, lines on a palm or oracle cards, are launch sites to something beyond. The shapes, forms or textual meanings are the start rather than the end of the journey. So, when you turn to the guidebook stories and one-minute messages for this oracle, *loosen your gaze*. Let the facts and dictionary meanings become a little hazy as they are not nearly as relevant here as feeling and suggestion. They are but doorways.

Understanding the details and exactitudes is not as important as what you sense the card stories mean to you in the moment. Allow their messages to change depending on who you are at the time of reading (or who you are reading for).

All the best on your sagacious adventures with *Maxine Gadd's Zoologica: The Steampunk Oracle*. Enjoy!

Leela J. Williams

A TREATISE ON THE USE OF THIS ORACLE FOR DIVINATION, CONTEMPLATION AND INSPIRATION

Imagination Is Not Just the Beginning

Whether you wish to glimpse the future, your soul, a solution or a story idea, come to this deck without assumptions. A fresh page holds the most possibilities, and an approach free of judgement, preconceptions and hypotheses will allow cogs to turn and sparks to fly beyond your current awareness and consideration.

Rather than focussing on situations, read for your past, current and future selves. Even when you don't relate to a card or a creature, try on their perspective. Play around in their realm to see how it feels. This will help you assess any insights and intuitions the cards prompt objectively.

Welcome mistakes and misinterpretations and impossibilities as part of your process. I've found that being absolutely willing to veer wildly off-track can be incredibly helpful to the divination process. Value learning, adaptability and responsiveness over getting things right. Try releasing the idea that things will stay as they are or work themselves out without too much bother before every reading.

By doing this, you ask more of yourself, life and your cards. Believing in and planning for a wonderful future can take practice. Put the effort in!

One of the best readings I have ever experienced laid out a direly unappealing future. I'd been offered several opportunities, all of which looked interesting and exciting. The cards revealed a pattern within those offers that closely reflected the work environment I aimed to move away from. It was humbling to see how easily I could fall into the same old situation if I didn't take responsibility and set some clear boundaries within myself. With further insight and support, I was able to reject that patterning and do something completely different.

That anecdote is a reminder that what seems realistic to you on any given day will likely be a false limit. To gaze beyond that boundary, jump out of your comfort zone. Taking that bold leap into wondrous possibility is much easier when you have a safe place to return to. Anchor yourself to a quality or memory where you feel secure, then stretch into whimsy, fantasy and what actually could be if (like the beings of this deck) you made a tweak here and an adjustment there, tightened a pulley or released a lever. The mechanics of change are mostly about adapting and fine-tuning existing designs. We rarely need to reinvent the wheel – and when we do, it's always an interesting ride.

Shuffling into Liminal Space

Whichever method you use for shuffling and selecting cards is completely fine. Be comfortable and curious. Blowing a raspberry, reciting a nursery rhyme and skipping in a circle can create liminal space as they get you out of your head and into the profound and outrageous sense of the unlimited moment. You can invite crystals, incense, charms, Cheshire Cats, top hats and timekeepers to your divination party. You may prefer a more intimate setting of just you and your cards. I will make no prescription other than to play with your preferences and be ready to listen.

The Art of the Pose (Wording Your Question)

You don't have to have a question. Anytime you feel drawn to draw a card, reach for your deck and do it. The message will speak to an aspect of your soul, your day or your imagination.

When there is something specific you would like the cards to address, you still don't need to ask a question. However, relating the message to a question can help with interpretation. Begin with the first question that pops into your head or one that has been rolling around in your mind all afternoon. But before you present it to your cards, consider whether it is talking to the core of your query.

Is the question open or closed? Closed questions have simple answers. They often have a limited number of short-answer responses, so they can be good when looking for a direct answer. Open questions elicit more nuanced, less specific answers. They can reveal more complexity and detail. These types of questions can deepen and broaden your understanding of a situation or yourself.

I prefer to focus my questions on what I can control ... as in, on me. That means they never involve anyone else. "Will Sherlock solve this mystery?" is a passive question. "Will I find a solution to this mystery?" is a closed question. "What can I do to deepen my understanding of this mystery?" is an open question that puts me in the action. I believe that the best readings are those that put you at the centre as an enthusiastic participant.

And so shines a good reading in a weary world ...

Pathways to Meaning

The inner workings of how and why we ascribe meaning to something are mysterious, subjective and deeply personal. A repeated image, a familiar phrase, synchronicity or random titbits that spring a distant memory into clear focus in the present can elevate the mundane to significance. With this understanding, the Zoologica offer an array of discovery processes and pathways to meaning.

Intuitive: Do It Your Way

This pathway involves going with what you know of the animals, the number on the cards and any details that jump out from the card text and images. For this process, disregard the guidebook, lean into your intuition and notice any responses that arise in your mind, heart or body. Pay attention to your first impressions and be ready to challenge them, as this can be a good way to recognise where you are now and where you might prefer to be.

Interpretive: Story Time

Each character of the Zoologica has a story to tell. When you meet a card for the first, second, third or hundredth time, you might like to turn to the guidebook and imbibe its tale. As stories, these card messages are open to interpretation. Your understanding of them will be influenced by your question, your mood, your perspective, your situation and more.

Read the stories from start to finish and swing back to any sections you feel drawn to re-examine. Pay attention to any words that jump out or seem awkward. Phrases that evoke feeling or remind you of a person or situation could hold particular relevance. Some ideas won't resonate with you at all, and you might brush over them entirely. Thus, the messages will be revealed through an intuitive process of elimination and illumination. This pathway guides your intuition while allowing it to explore and discover fresh meaning in the cards with every reading.

Definitive: One-Minute Messages

For direct answers that don't require intuition or interpretation, turn to the one-minute messages. These meanings are all together in a section of their own after the card stories, so you don't need to go flicking back and forth through the guidebook. This also gives the card stories their own space, so your intuitive interpretations are not influenced by the one-minute messages. While you may notice some overlap with the stories, these sections are distinct.

Immersive: Every Witch Way You Choose

Yes! Of course, you can combine the intuitive, interpretative and definitive processes for a multi-dimensional perspective on the same query. You might like to tune in to the card characters and ask them to share or inspire other stories, poetry or artworks. As you get to know the Zoologica, you will naturally ascribe each creature with qualities, feelings and situations. Play with and listen to them – and use your journal to keep track of the outcomes.

THE LAYING DOWN OF CARDS

Using a card spread will help give your readings a beginning, a middle and a clear ending. You'll also be able to compare outcomes and make connections between times, options and influences – depending on the spread. Use the following spreads, your trusted favourites or develop your own steampunk-themed layouts.

One-Card Whizzard

A single-card reading can be the simplest path to a direct answer. However, it does put pressure on that one card to deliver a concise and accurate message. The steampunk Zoologica are up to the task. Ask your question, shuffle and select a card in the method of your choosing. Commit to your question and commit to receiving an answer from the card you choose.

First, consider the nature of the response as indicated by the habitat of the being depicted on the card. Creatures that can move between domains invite a broader focus than a being of a single element. For example, *Tree Frog* can move from water to earth to tree and will be addressing more elements of your world than the water-bound *Oranda Goldfish*. Also, consider the heights and depths of the habitat. A creature of the abyssal zone speaks to deeper emotions than that of coastal shallows.

Water: Emotion
On the earth: Body
In the earth: Subconscious Mind
Tree: Conscious Mind
Sky: Spirit

Once you have identified the element or zone the card represents, invite that aspect (or aspects) of yourself to respond to the image. Note any feelings that arise. Then turn to the one-minute meaning and relate the message to your question. When you are ready, explore the answer further through the card's story.

You may have chosen to draw a single card because you are looking for an instant answer, but a clear response may not be immediate. Put your question aside and trust clarity to come to you within the coming day or night. A relaxed, unhurried mind gifts space for insight.

The Trinity Effect

Once is random, twice is a coincidence, thrice is a pattern. It takes three points to triangulate an exact location. So, a three-card reading can reveal where you are, how you came to be here and what will likely happen next. Recognising and understanding the key influence on the pattern that brought you to this moment can help you change your current trajectory. If you want to change it!

Card One: The questioner in the present in relation to the question.

Card Two: A key influence on the current query.

Card Three: The most likely outcome – if the current pattern is unbroken.

The Tick Tock Revelation

This layout plays with the idea that life is not a linear journey from Point A to Point B, but a concentric relationship between all points in time. We can move the dials, shift the cogs, refine the mechanism and change the clock face. How we experience our circles of influence determines how we perceive ourselves and our possibilities. There is no time like now for a soul-shifting revelation.

1. Ask your question, shuffle, choose five cards and lay them face down in any order per the diagram.

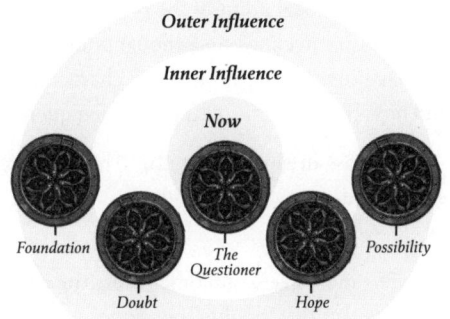

2. Turn the cards and read them one by one. You can move from the inner point outward, the outer point inward or in any other order you wish.

   Foundation: The underlying principles, beliefs or values on which a question or situation is raised. This card refers to building blocks, such as circumstances or experiences that brought you to the present quandary.

   Doubt: This card can identify where a supportive boost could quickly contribute to meaningful change. Identify and replace any limiting self-talk with compassion and encouragement.

   The Questioner: A focal point of the reading, this card connects to the core identity, feelings and thoughts of the person being read for. It may provide insight into their characteristics, attitude, energy and how they view the situation being queried.

   Hope: Aspirations, dreams and faith. This card reveals areas where healing and opportunity are desired and approached with optimism.

   Possibility: The most likely outcome where the current patterns, energies, beliefs, actions, doubts and hopes are left to run their current course, uninterrupted.

3. Once all the cards have been revealed, explore the relationship between all the points of your journey.

4. Delve into these connections further by asking which qualities or lessons you would reinforce, which you would change, and which you would remove.

5. Now, rearrange the cards in the order of your choosing, per the second diagram.

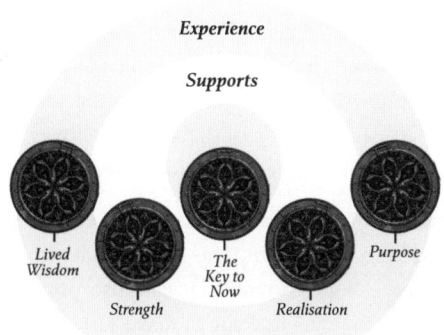

6. Read the cards in any order, delve into these meanings and explore the connections between them as you did previously.

Lived Wisdom: Knowledge gained through direct experience. This card talks of valuable lessons and insights that are known with your whole self (heart, body and mind). Lived wisdom can be instinctive, practical, resourceful and resilient – and unacknowledged. Claim it!

Strength: Areas where you have tackled the tough stuff and become confident, flexible and empowered. A little success leads to further success, so this card identifies areas where improvement, growth and courage are imminent.

The Key to Now: This card is about having the insight, clarity and motivation to drive the present into the tomorrow of your choosing. It can identify actions, perspectives, feelings and supports to prioritise for a positive outcome.

Realisation: A confirmation or reminder of what can be manifested from the present. This card can identify what it might take to bring a hope to reality. It can also provide a profound understanding that will free you to make a positive move.

Purpose: Committed and chosen direction. This card represents a transformation from 'perhaps' or 'maybe' into a clear, self-actualised goal and sense of meaning.

Your lived wisdom, strengths, realisations and purpose may be in process, unfinished, but powerfully on their way to becoming the key to your current query. Feel a positive shift ripple across your timeline as you realise you can draw insight and empowerment from your past, your present and your future.

Clarifiers

Answers can lead to more questions, so it can be handy to add a clarifying card to your spread. This card can lend understanding, confidence or depth to a reading. You can draw a clarifier for any card or spread. I recommend drawing only one clarifier for simple spreads (up to five cards) and two for more complex layouts. Otherwise, the core message of your reading can be diluted or lost.

As a support card, the role of the clarifier is to nudge, highlight or accentuate an element of the original card. Avoid overthinking the meaning of the clarifying card. Run with the first feeling, word or phrase that jumps out from the image or text.

If you still feel unclear about the message, try rephrasing your question, reshuffling and trying another spread. Or you can walk away from your question and the reading and trust your intuitive process is already at work and will reveal your answer in a powerful and surprising way over the course of your day and night.

1. GALAGO
Darkness Be Thy Playground

There may be an earthen path that requires no more than one steady footfall ahead of another to make it through this darkness. If it exists at all, it was lost along with the light. You can stumble through a ground maze until you chance across it. Or, you can **say farewell to two-dimensional progress**, don your night goggles, oil your joints, and bound upward **to** transform the night forest into your playground. Your pinpointed location may seem unchanged, but your new height will **transform your world completely**.

As you adjust your sights to the changing light, a clear course emerges. **The way is not straight and narrow** but a three-dimensional crisscross of ascents, leaps, drops, sidesteps and scurries punctuated by stillness and pause. In these quiet moments, taken at the peaks of your journey, you survey your surroundings and plot the next sequence from each branch, trunk and cluster to the next.

You rest, observe and ponder so that when a pipe, not as strong as expected, snaps under your weight, **you have the momentum, flexibility and reach to land safely** on another.

The darkness obscures all that lies beneath you, but you leap with faith in yourself, knowing that with each firm hold, you already have the impetus to reach for the next. When you fall, it is always forward. When you come to the ground, it is nimbly, from the lowest of the branches, and you are soon scooting up the nearest rise to **your elevated perspective** once more. Your progress may be swift and surprising but never panicked or erratic. The steam-filled canopy **provides safe holds where you can** catch your breath and carefully **consider your next** series of **moves**.

Travel light to keep your hands and mind free. You may feel you are leaving something behind, be it an ability, an interest, a friendship, an opportunity or a part of yourself. However, it is not abandoned but parked. You'll be able to swing back and pick up what you left off once you have explored your new surroundings. Somewhere amidst your backs and forths and ups and downs, you join a network of night navigators, softly and effortlessly helping others through their own darkness.

2. CARPENTER BEE
The Constant Buzz is Golden

The breath of winter, the icy touch you retreated from, wanes and submits to the burgeoning light. As the steam's promise dallies ever longer and higher in the sky, warmth seeps back into the world, enlivening your heart, your joints and your desire for sweetness. The space you drilled into for comfort and restful solitude now feels stifling and small. It is devoid of the golden particles so diligently stored away before the coldness descended. All that gold has now been integrated into your being, smoothing over scratches and dents and renewing your shine. **Emerge from your hideaway and** feel the new wind's invitation to dance.

The world is big, exciting and fraught with unexpected challengers. When confronted, doubted or blocked, you **choose presence over force**. Your buzz announces your intention, creates openings and dislodges golden dust from inaccessible places. In time, you will find a partner with whom you can share the labours of your shared purpose, but for now, you **embark on your project** alone and undaunted. You carve out your niche **with simple tools and small, consistent actions**.

Retreat has its season and reasons. You have absorbed all you can in isolation. Put what you've learned toward your pursuit of sweetness. Avoidance will not bring you to your gold. **Spread your wings and trust** their small, reliable movement to carry you. Their vibration protects, propels and shakes up your environment for the better.

You carry more wisdom than it seems possible to have collected within the time you've had. This is the harvest of consistency. Every tiny lesson, revelation and gratitude compound to create a fuller sweetness that nurtures you and your endeavours in colder times. Ideas are pollinated, and connections and openings are made as you move from one golden source to another. Feel the warmth in your wings and buzz!

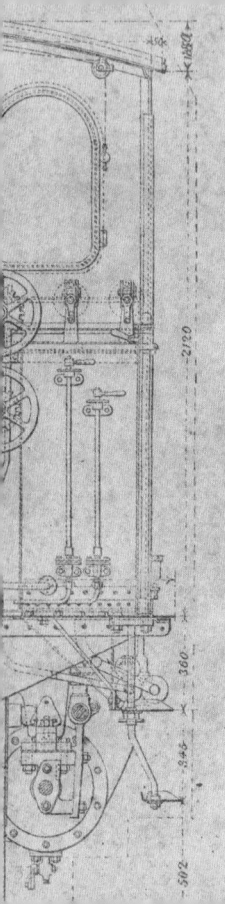

It's still magic,
even if you know how it's done.

-Terry Pratchett,
'A Hat Full of Sky'

3. ANGLERFISH
Symbionic Strategy

Deep below the waterline, there are magics and imaginings. Adapting to this strange territory requires unique mechanisms. The quiet here magnifies movement, and you are fiercely aware of the shifts in your surroundings. You journey with a light of your own making, but its glow is an attractor, not a guide. Would-be mates, nurturers and predators come to this dangling beacon, distracted, curious and disarmed by novelty. You are **happy to be misunderstood and underestimated** while you make your assessment – is this being friend or foe?

You are fascinated by those who are enthralled by your light. You observe their charms, vulnerabilities, protections and interactions and absorb them all. **You choose what to show of yourself** while closely studying the responses of those in your spotlight. At a hint of judgement or cruelty, the retreat to shadows can be so swift it will be as if what was revealed never existed. But you remember the reactions, the micro-expressions and the changes in tone that preceded them. There is no 'next time' as you recognise the signs of trouble earlier than most.

You **test and trial and incorporate all you learn into your** current strategies. Even the most skilfully **craft**ed mechanisms have their limits, and when you reach yours, you will mine all you have witnessed to modify your systems. Your fallback is logic and independence. While you are tentative to **trust, you are part of the whole**. All you feel, all you know, even your light, are the result of symbiotic connections.

There is no usual response to an atypical situation or environment. Ingenious mechanisms support you as you learn to recognise, navigate and respond to threats. Through these same processes, you build confidence in your ability to identify the wonders in the weirdness of the world. Time is your friend. There will be those who see you and let you see them. Perhaps you have found them already. They may have had their own strange journeys and developed ways of taking on a world that seemed bigger than themselves. In this way, an ever-growing number of select beings will swim and adapt with you and add to your light.

4. PRAYING MANTIS
The Patience of Purpose

Amidst the whir and whiz, the fast-paced and flourishing, a drama of sound, scent and colour vies for attention. The brighter, the louder and the wittier distract and enthral. While all eyes and ears are upon them, **you are free to roam, explore and plan at your leisure**. You are so at one with your surroundings, quietly and elegantly setting your sights on your next destination, your next achievement, that **your advancement goes unseen** and, thus, unchallenged. Under the cover of ordinary, you have the luxury of **unhurried, measured and watchful** progress. You have blended in, are part of the foliage, but **you are far from ordinary**.

You are not renowned for your entrances, but when the spotlight chances your way, you do not disappoint. When someone does take notice, they seem surprised that you've been here all along (even when you just arrived) and wonder how they never noticed your exquisite wings. You may then lull their curiosity, and so humbly camouflage your differences that the inattentive and preoccupied soon lose interest and leave you to your own devices. Those who continue to suspect **there is more to you than meets the eye** are right. When you can avoid a challenger, you will. You don't like to reveal your hand too early, but when pressed, you show your strengths quickly and decisively.

You are exacting because you have observed the great detail of your surroundings. You know what you want, the skills needed to get there and the opponents, traps and distractions you will encounter. Your **patience and preparedness** mean you see and are **ready** for opportunity and adversity. You are rarely shocked. Though **you** might be still, you are not stunned but poised. When you strike, it is with honed precision, timed **for the highest chance of success**.

In your quiet self, you contemplate the turning of the cogs and the ups and downs of their players. The plans you make in the background of your world are your own. They are often beyond what others may deem you capable of, but you are not here to impress with fast and showy results. Yours is the long, winding and satisfying path taken with unassuming persistence, calm awareness and startling ability. Your success may stun the hummingbird, but all the leaves of the grove cheer, as they knew you as their own.

I like to imagine that the world is one big machine. You know, machines never have any extra parts. They have the exact number and type of parts they need. So I figure if the entire world is a big machine, I have to be here for some reason. And that means you have to be here for some reason, too.

-Brian Selznick,
'The Invention of Hugo Cabret'

5. MEERKAT
Mischief of a Higher Order

Oh, what a high hat you have! You tip it to those you pass with a twinkle in your eye and a flurry of your step. Your preened nod to the establishment lets them believe they know and have it all while stating your lofty position outside conventionality. You mock and lightly rock the cogs of the system while nudging and tweaking it to your benefit. It is not the machine but the values it is organised around that attract your ridicule. And while, on occasion, you may muse that the system runs on fools, not fuels, you have no issue with the individuals who give themselves to proving their worth. It is **by luck and circumstance** that **you know another way**.

Parallel to the material chase is an alternative mode of existence where beings have nothing to prove. You exist, and therefore, you belong. In this close-knit, loose-fitting community, backs are scratched before an itch arises. Long hands and short, move with a reliable tick and comforting tock to **care** for the vulnerable **and**

prepare for the heat and the dry. Invisible bonds, unspoken covenants and shared resources bind your collective against falsity or misused power.

And today, you are off **to make good mischief**. Perhaps as an interloper, loosening a screw and redirecting a nozzle to add a little warmth to the cold and the humourless. Perhaps as an agitator or a petitioner diplomatically dipping a quill in the well of change. You are unattached to your role. Should you be called elsewhere tomorrow, you could wear another hat just as well. You are not your airs, your graces or your expertise. All of these you will gladly shed and share, for **when you prosper**, your community (however small or large) grows with you. When **your community grows**, you prosper with it. That is the secret of that twinkle in your eye.

You may feel like an interloper–in a system, but not of it–distanced from your people or your values. Spend your time there to your advantage. Learn the many ways to make light work and the work lighter. The hat doesn't wear you. While you wear it, open the lofty cap to voices that are sweet and true. Sing together to invoke the covenant of community, and don't lose sight of the greater mischief. You will come to wear other hats and no hat at all, and all you learn, all you gain, and all you change, will benefit you and yours in all ways.

6. NAUTILUS
Emotional Ballast

It's coming around again. However long the cycle, these upwellings and currents will always be familiar when they return. Your very being recalls it, and your reaction is innate. This memory is not baggage but ballast. It is not a load to bear but a fount of balance, buoyancy and brilliance. **You know how to navigate these waters**. Once upon a time, you were at the mercy of the tide, but now you sift and shift the weight of your experience to find your way with grace while augmenting your wisdom in successive spirals.

You are in control of your emotional ballast. You know how to draw into your lower chambers when it's time to go deep, how to expand into levity and what to release to **propel yourself** through **and** away from troubled waters. You can do this because you have juggled, jiggled, pushed and pulled all you carry through your inner chambers, examining it, aerating it, never letting it settle and harden into a fixed narrative or lower esteem. You know what you can throw off and the elements you can pull together to **direct your movement**.

Those who only see your outer shell would marvel at the elegance of your inner workings. Your nuanced and gentle responses make it seem like you float through chaos effortlessly. They don't see all the times and tides you've known. You've been buoyed by sophisticated strategies born of avoidance, worry, and finally, acceptance. And now, **you see what is coming** in advance, **and have the resources** and equilibrium **to** stay steady or re-**route your course as you wish**.

As a submariner, you experience the world on a deeper level. Those on the surface may not understand the richness you encounter. Multi-dimensional living can be scary, overwhelming and complex, but for you, any other approach would feel shallow and unfulfilling. Though it can take a little longer to process and find your balance in your surroundings, this is your world. The spirals you create here have golden ratios and jewelled chambers that help you manoeuvre your emotional ballast to ride the currents while growing your capacity and sagacity.

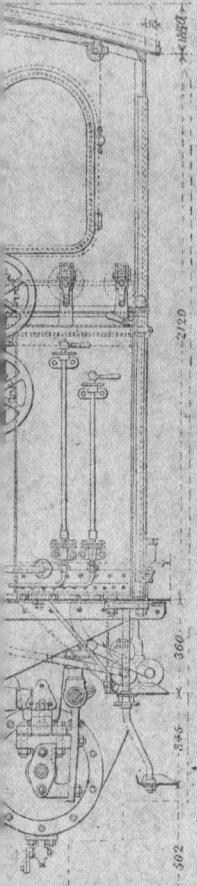

Perhaps there's another, much larger story behind the printed one, a story that changes just as our own world does. And the letters on the page tell us only as much as we'd see peering through a keyhole. Perhaps the story in the book is just the lid on the pan; it always stays the same, but underneath there's a whole world that goes on developing and changing like our own.

-Cornelia Funke,
'Inkspell'

7. HOUSE WREN
Fuelled by Movement

The first feather of dawn tickles at your to-do list, and you are up and away. There are ticks and checks and boxes and so much more you're set to give your attention to today. The tiniest errand is part of a grander plan, each delightful detail a mark of gratitude and every joyous 'just so' is a commitment to the moment and the momentous. You are fuelled by movement. Flapping and spinning from fix to task keeps your batteries charged. **The more you do, the more efficient you become and the more energy you have**.

Your high activity is matched by your mental acuity. Schedules and responsibilities for your career, home, family, volunteer work and vacations come together like a like complex, multi-functional machinery. Any leverage created in one area is utilised in another. If there is a way to fulfil two birds with one honed action, you will find it! You flitter between projects and attend to the unexpected so effortlessly that others, even yourself, can forget how much planning and tweaking and oiling goes into making everything run so smoothly.

When a spanner is thrown or a flap unhinged, you pull strings and tighten connections to keep cogs turning. **There is time** for one more task, one last tweak and one final measure before the sun sets and then … you rest. And you **rest well**. Be it unwinding with a book, a partner or a pet, you nestle into the comforts of your choice, sleep soundly, dream deeply **and recharge**.

Many plans make lighter work. You love lining things up and seeing them fall into place. One interest or focus is rarely enough to satisfy your attention. Refining your mechanisms frees up time that is quickly filled with fresh pursuits – ensure they are your own. Your energy remains limitless, with a few conditions. Guard your downtime. When night falls, unplug your busy mind and body and let the measure of your nest be the quality of your rest.

8. DRAGONFLY
Warming Up For Genius

Delicate, polydexterous and able to carry your weight in gold? **Yes!** Those wings, your means of upliftment, are a brazen display of design genius. They flap, rotate and tilt so **you can** fly up, down, forward, back and sideways – in slow motion or high speed. You can **take** sharp turns and hover silently in one place. Once something is in **your** sights (as is often the case due to your wide and multi-focal lenses), you have the skill and agility to chase any fanciful flight. Your wings even energise you as they move. You are a keen-visioned, self-propelling aeronautical extraordinaire!

Once you get started …

This style of genius takes **time** to warm up. In the fresh face of the morning, you find an unassuming position where you can bask in the sunlight without drawing attention to yourself. You are vulnerable, for now, and happy to be overlooked. You watch, quiet and unmoving, except for the gentle shift of wings as they redirect the solar rays to power your engines. In this stillness, you **study** your surroundings, stretching your focus to **the horizon** and mentally rehearsing your flight.

And what a flight it will be! Just imagine the wind in your wings as you breeze across brooks, dart into the distance and rise to new heights. There is to be no early start, so enjoy your reverie. Watch the interplay of the morning and see yourself zooming along with the comings and goings of the day. The warmth is already weaving through your coils, and **your motor will soon be firing**.

Attempting to take off with a cold engine won't get you far. One or two false starts are more than okay. However, you soon learn that waiting until your wings are whirring, whizzing and charged for flight makes for a more impressive and confident launch. Once in the air, you'll be self-powered. Genius will not be rushed. Relax, absorb the light of your surroundings and feel it empower you. It will soon be your moment to dazzle.

9. PUFFER FISH
Havens in the Sand

Amidst shifting sands and perpetual currents, how does the fresh and fragile develop without being buried, disrupted or washed away? Birthing the new and surprising in such an unaccommodating world seems futile. It is impossible to hold back the tide and naïve to wait for the perfect conditions. So, **ideas are** lost or tucked away, and their carriers become elusive but not despondent. They move with the tides, **waiting and watching for** a little **encouragement and a safe place** to land. Creating that environment is a true work of art. A nudge and a furrow here, an inspired repurposing of resources there, a redirection of currents there … and voila!

These spaces are sheltered, guarded and beautiful. They are also temporary. Your castles in the sand will be lost to time, but the **hope and reassurance** they offer **endure**. They are pockets of safety, not just for ideas and idealists, but for secrets, doubts, unburdening and more. Weeks and more have gone into building this moment of trust, and it is precious. You are the catalyst for this freeing. You do all you can to **welcome** and provide a serene environment for **the new** to develop from embryo to independence, but it is not yours to hold. Only by facing the open tides will the once hidden become truly strong and free.

Like many skilled and patient artists, you prefer peace and a quiet life where you can ponder the full palette of resources naturally at your disposal. You are too focused on providing transformative spaces to seek out trouble or start chaos. This can be mistaken for weakness or false optimism, making you look like an easy target. However, your drive to create is born from realism. You know **the world can be harsh** and **sanctuary is blessed**. You do not engage in combat, competition and other pursuits of the foolish. Rather, you baffle your assailants and detractors with a grandiose show of authority and poise. There is no need to retaliate, as **your presence speaks for itself**.

You may see yourself as a quiet and consistent catalyst or an usher for change. However, it is your calm and fierce response to challengers that people remember. When push comes to shove, you are stoic. You never start or escalate a fight but are quick to shut them down. Those who misinterpret your modest nature and consideration for others as a vulnerability will quickly see your full measure. It isn't overly comfortable to gad around in grandeur all the time, but you are quick to make a show of your authority or sharp intellect to shut down an issue. It's a win for all. The aggressors step back before they get hurt, and you return to your preferred form, humbly engineering safe, welcoming and nurturing spaces where change is birthed.

10. WOMBAT
Propeller Head

Look closely at your creation and **be satisfied there is no trickery**. The framework, once a delicate fragment of imagination, has taken shape. It won't be believed, no matter how sincerely you explain. And convincing others won't make you sure, won't make it real. See your creation as though for the first time. Forget the days, weeks, months or years invested and pay it every scrutiny. Hunt for the weaknesses. Before you trust this glittering mechanism to **deliver** your future, there must be **substance in the fantastic**.

First impressions betray your speed, strength and determination. More considered observers might still question your diligence. When you appear to be doing nothing at all, the heaviest lifting goes on unseen in that most marvellous machine – your mind. The **transition from thought to reality** is fraught with fussing and fiddling (and cursing), but you dig in **and** stubbornly **defy** the **conventions** of what **you can** and can't do.

Under the bright burn of a lamp and your **magnify**ing lenses, you assess the cogs, springs and complications. Notes are checked, lists revisited, and though you've started over more than once, more than thrice, you'll do so again if that's what it takes. There is to be no trick of false confidence here. Groundbreaking daring and plodding critique are co-conspirators for **success**.

The innovations, ideas and thoughts that spin in one place cannot achieve lift-off. Move them out of your head and into the world where you can see and feel them more objectively. Test drive it all! In hearing something out loud, seeing it sketched out on paper, engineering the parts and piecing them together, you can sort the theory from the actual. Through trial and refinement, your framework takes form and becomes sturdy enough to carry you through. It is then time to take your seat at the helm, set your course and pull the lever. Hold tight – this ship is built to burst through glass ceilings!

"My mind," he said, "rebels at stagnation. Give me problems, give me work, give me the most abstruse cryptogram or the most intricate analysis, and I am in my own proper atmosphere. I can dispense then with artificial stimulants. But I abhor the dull routine of existence. I crave for mental exaltation. That is why I have chosen my own particular profession - or rather created it, for I am the only one in the world."

-Arthur Conan Doyle,
'The Sign of the Four'

11. CICADA
The Song That Gilds

Time rasps and cracks and bursts onto a golden afternoon. You have been waiting, growing, maturing, and you now glide through this open window. With wings polished, mechanisms wound and the pressure set to rise, you feel the fuel of urgency, knowing this dreamy weather cannot last. Over the threshold, you **march into the world** alight **with purpose** – emboldened by it!

There is no secret to be made of your intention. Hurry the connection by making your desires known. Raise your voice to those you meet, and they will become your allies. For what can one voice avail compared to three and more together? Sing loud, on your own and with others. You will not be lost in or deafened by the noise. You will **be heard**, and before too long, you will hear. The same breeze that wrote your chorus across the sky will carry an answering refrain to you.

Declare your dream loudly, and have your passion echoed back to you. Even a whisper is strengthened and multiplied as it works its way through pipelines, rattling poles and jumping contacts to reach a ready and charged network of support. Remember, **all you seek is seeking you**. Be seen, heard and found.

The events of this glimmering time will be hammered out with the help of connections not yet made. Dismiss any instinct to hide or diminish what you came here to do. Share your plans, collect business cards and follow up recommendations. Wherever you go, there is someone who knows someone who holds a puzzle piece you are looking for. Make some noise so you can find each other.

12. CHAMELEON
The Colour of Alchemy

The journey from lead to gold confounded and exhausted Science. It declared that metal could not be transmuted and mocked the invisible. But **behold!** Here, rising from the tip of a coiled tail, defying expectation, **something wondrous is taking place**. This is not corroding corrugations or a fleeting feat of cryptic colouration. You are not yet certain of the emerging shine – what it portends, if it will persist, and whether it is genuine. In truth, at times it seems that you scarcely know yourself, for everything is in flux, and with it, so too are you.

The modern alchemist seeks not to promise the impossible. Rather they peer into nature's hiding places and perform **tiny miracles of understanding**. When **accumulate**d, these minutiae can mimic thunder and earthquakes. Thus, mere acts of mortalkind venture into mythical territory. You are an unconscious alchemist – innately melding into situations and observing cause and effect, the traction, the sparks and the misfires. Your natural empathy and the intricate knowledge you garner gilds your ability to mimic and blend and so effortlessly shapeshift that you wonder whether the real you is substance or myth.

Nothing is lost in your alchemy. There are times for lead and others for gold. The transformation from one to the other is neither false nor fixed. You can be either or both or something else entirely – depending on what a situation calls for. **The real you is in control** of that decision, and if the result is mythical, so be it. You **choose what to** emulate and what alloys to **add to your toolkit**.

Think back to who you were this morning. No doubt you have changed several times since then as you don the colours of your private self, your social self, your curious self, your waiting-to-see-what-is-expected self and more. The more adeptly you adapt to your environment, the more you may wonder who you are at your core – who are you without reaction and outside influence? Choose who you are to be, and remember, all that glistens can one day be gold.

13. SEA JELLIES
Orchestrated Ease

Oh, spellbinding traveller, may **the tides of fortune bless you**. For surely one so calm in the current is at its mercy? The elegance of your wave dance, with its fanciful fluctuations, lulls the observer to believe you arrived here by chance. But it is by your design, not a whim of destiny. You marked this spot, charted your course, and here you are with the keys to your treasure.

When a tricky tide arises, you face it with the practised poise and measured beat of a maestro. You draw from the future to propel you from the past with rhythmic efficiency, leaving trails of protection and carrying the keys. You can do all that and more and still have the energy to shine. Your luminescence (a light in troubled waters!) adds to the mesmeric nature of your swift and steady progress.

You do make it look easy. Those who navigate these waters alongside you know what it takes. But others cannot appreciate the breadth of your efforts or the **small joys** that **fuel** you. It seems you are coasting along on pomp and circumstance rather than by pump and **purpose**. How do they not see your constant and diligent actions? They are on view in plain sight but interpreted as art, a pursuit of pleasure or a savant's quirk. All of which are free of tedium and deliberation and thus undeserving of thanks or treasures. And any gains they bring are happy accidents – *do not believe this!* **Your happiness is no accident**.

Making the complex seem simple and a load look light can work for and against you. Finessed and carefully planned outcomes may be mistaken for inevitable results. When you are floating along with apparent ease, there is a temptation to add one more link in your chain, manage one more tangle or carry one more passenger. Unusual vigour is truly living light – but it is not limitless. Those who share that light know that nothing comes from nothing. They care for each other, share the fuel of gratitude and recognition, and encourage each other not to take on the expectations or responsibilities of others. Carry the keys to your treasure and orchestrate your dazzling success.

14. LITTLE BROWN BAT
Navigate the Now

An inventory of instruments has begun. Considering the current conditions, it is no surprise the compass needles are acting wildly. The tuning forks are pitched to the sounds of first light. While darkness is queen, you can put them aside with your hypsometer and sextant and turn to other aids. The wind would make a mockery of your maps and charts, but you have poured over this terrain so often that you can recall its detail without assistance. **In the** sudden **shock of the storm**, both your position and direction were lost. But all you need **is a clue**, one landmark or constellation, and you'll know where you are.

The echoes of past, future and what was present are fuzzy, but if you adjust your stance, you can make out the points you need to triangulate your position. This is not a simple task while lightning disrupts the night, thunder rolls through the valleys, and wind roils the water. **This tempest was designed to confuse**. In the gaps between outbursts, you find your bearings and begin to plot your course home.

You need not wait for the storm to subside, as your humble wings can elevate you to dazzling heights. You can **journey above and be**yond the cacophonous clouds – as soon as you know where you are. Without that clear starting point, any flight will be baffling and misdirected. So, wait for the percussion to rest and feel into **the stillness** to find your pointers.

Storm makers can time their chaos for deliberate and dramatic effect. The tumult can put you off kilter, so you lose your sense of place and self. Resist caving to the shock of the moment. You can process what you need once you have found your way to safety. Dust off your tools and assess which ones you can rely on in the current circumstances. Triangulate your position and free yourself into the heights of calm.

"As for difficulties," replied Ferguson, in a serious tone, "they were made to be overcome; as for risks and dangers, who can flatter himself that he is to escape them? Everything in life involves danger; it may even be dangerous to sit down at one's own table, or to put one's hat on one's own head. Moreover, we must look upon what is to occur as having already occurred, and see nothing but the present in the future, for the future is but the present a little farther on."

-Jules Verne,
'Five Weeks in a Balloon'

15. HOUSE FLY
The Tea Cup Flows Over, Unspilled

The tea has been steeped to perfection and served with all the finery one would expect. You, unassuming, take note of the beverage's flavour and the character of those who partake. As the scandal is shared and drama declared, it is done so with the trimmings of Shakespeare. Hyperbole and conjecture create **much ado about nothing**. The subjects of the tale are not here to confirm or deny the events and accusations. Thus, the story may grow and spread, unchecked and untroubled by the hurt it could cause.

The tale does not conclude with the clearing of the tea set and the departure of the guests. The glow of the gathering will be recounted, its details travelling through letters and along metal wires, perhaps even finding its way into the gossip columns. The allure of a captivating story means that truth needn't get in the way. Yet, for those who must confront false claims and wonder at how such a rumour could have taken flight, there will be no solace. Therefore, you take action to stop it before it grows wings and takes off into the world.

You are quick to see a tale for the power it holds. With your sharp wit and keen understanding, you are fast to **discern the intent** behind the buzz **and** fly in to nimbly **redirect** a conversation towards happier ends. With a deft touch and a clever turn of phrase, **idle chatter** is transformed into a meaningful exchange filled **with empathy, kindness and genuine connection**.

As a mere observer, you can unlock the secrets of the soul, piecing together heart-led portrayals of humans and their foibles. You see the power held within all the buzz we share with each other. Charitable thinking, attentive listening and supportive language can nourish our connections and circles. Gossip and malice cannot be returned to the pot. However, you can hover around the honey of kindness and compassion, directing people to sweeter truths and creating a better world, one conversation at a time.

16. TORTOISE
Your Story, Your Pace

How can one finish if they never begin? Oh, but your start was made long ago. Your wisdom and protections were forged in iron and sealed with ancient copper. Their weight may slow you, but **there is no pleasure in** the **rush**. Besides, you have such a head start – it will be some time before the world catches up.

Some lives can be lived many times over and thrice times again. Those who good-naturedly hint that the hours are wasting encounter your wry smile. Just last week, you dined with a dodo and shared morning tea with a blauwbok. Last night the quagga made a sport of charades and this twilight may welcome a Caspian tiger – perhaps with a Tasmanian friend? What is remembered is not lost. And the **memories** of your adventures through the best and worst of times **make fine company** while you wait.

The heroes of these reveries (former and ever-present aspects of yourself) are indeed your friends. They are naïve, reckless, unwitting or driven to folly. Or questioning, earnest, studious or humbled. Or curious, brave, reluctant or magnificently ablaze with impassioned pursuit. And now, they are restful, reflective and patiently **wait**ing ... **for the world to catch up** and present you with a fresh and worthy venture.

Those who recognise your contentment, your peace with your selves, may wonder at your secrets. However, their supplications will not hasten the flow of your tongue. When you recount your tales, it is by the power of your discretion to those who may benefit from the telling. You share with equal parts caution and delight, knowing your listener may still choose to learn–even the most difficult lessons–for themselves. You don't owe anyone your story. It is yours to tell at your pace. And it isn't over – gosh, it's barely begun!

17. KOALA
Scarlet Studies

Following clues and unravelling mysteries requires **a steadfast commitment to** reason. One must remain ever vigilant against the intrusion of tempers, lest they impose upon your delicate investigations. **Conclusions** must be **drawn with** care, devoid of bias or the influence of false witness and dubious testimony. It is through the lens of deliberate, logical and dispassionate observations that you gain clarity. Dust cannot distort your **high-powered** lenses, nor can emotions muddy your **understanding**.

Magnifying the need for precision and objectivity, the matter that has intrigued your focus is oft described as lost, hopeless and irrelevant. Yet, you continue to sift through facts and scrutinise memories. The task is arduous, but you are unready and unwilling to put it aside. As **another clue comes to light**, your hat and temperament are wound for accuracy. And the scarlet threads of feeling are hastily wrapped in silk and secured under lock and key.

When the matter at hand is solved and resolved, you can bring out the ornate box, unfold the silk, and the contents shall unravel in unpredictable patterns that re-colour your world. Should you choose (and you will), these weavings can be brought under your magnifier. They will not intrude upon nor cast doubt on your reasoning, but they may confirm or challenge your findings. While you can detach from their mercurial influence, you know it is unwise to overlook **your emotions**. They can **hold the greatest clues of all**.

A fresh clue has set your mind ticking. This new trigger may hold the key to a cipher, so you revisit past ground, discounting or bolstering theories or opening startling lines of inquiry. You can talk about the case with cool disinterest. Others may find this a curious habit, but you fear that hope, disappointment or anger may cloud and derail your inner process. Stepping back from the quandary, and depersonalising it, helps you see the pieces and how they fit together. You do know this puzzle may be unsolvable and cannot be reasoned away. However, looking at it with dedicated reason brings you ever closer to understanding, accepting and trusting your feelings. That's what this detective work is all about.

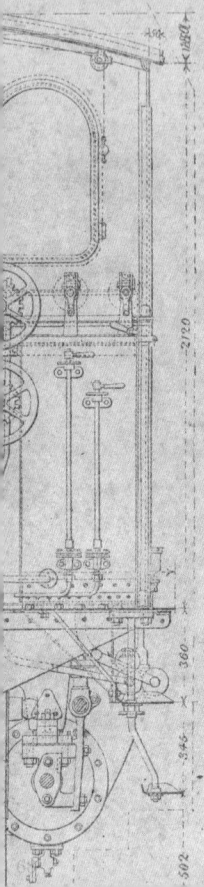

"Facts," murmured Basil, like one mentioning some strange, far-off animals, "how facts obscure the truth. I may be silly—in fact, I'm off my head—but I never could believe in that man—what's his name, in those capital stories?—Sherlock Holmes. Every detail points to something, certainly; but generally to the wrong thing. Facts point in all directions, it seems to me, like the thousands of twigs on a tree. It's only the life of the tree that has unity and goes up—only the green blood that springs, like a fountain, at the stars."

—G.K. Chesterton,
'The Club of Queer Trades'

18. SPANNER CRAB
The Unfixed

It is not expected that the amateur should comprehend the intricate nuances of your strange trade. There are labours and studies, perils and consultations that go unnoticed, unseen by the untrained eye. Perhaps the more curious onlooker may muster a modicum of understanding, but they only skim the surface. They know nothing of how the problem came into your capable hands, nor do they fully comprehend the sophisticated workings of the mechanism you are tasked to restore. For those who remain content to call it magic, know this: **the truth is** far more **complex** than mere sorcery.

The nuts and bolts are simple enough. Undeveloped, neglected or unmotivated talent only hints at what could be. When an **innate ability** is **coupled with** a **driving interest**, it **is a fortunate occurrence**. Manuals and treatises, so dull to the uninitiated, become intriguing companions and trusted guides. Savants of your trade, bearers of oft-misunderstood genius, are co-conspirators in your pursuit of joy. And we've not yet touched on the magic.

The alchemy is in your approach. Something in your ornate manner, your keen focus and your open fascination put people at ease. You see not what is before you but what could be. As you speak, your words encapsulate this magic, so others begin to see as you do. They might not know how it will happen, but enthralled by your enthusiastic vision, they believe it can be. That belief changes the broken into **something that** just **needs a little adjustment**. Tweaked and redirected, parts that were faulty, draining or useless **will become** whole **new sources of energy** and functionality.

Here, in your capable hands, is a strange problem that requires an unusual fix. The first tool to call on is daring. This is the kinetic force that will charge your optimism and confidence. Connect these internal devices to your vision. Dare to see not what is before you but what it can be. From there, throw your spanners into the works. The broken is unfixed (changing and variable). With practical know-how and effort, you can give it the nudge it needs so everything falls into place. It is not quite like before. The space it has cleverly fallen into, the position it now holds, comes with improved performance, durability and some surprising enhancements.

Even broken in spirit as he is, no one can feel more deeply than he does the beauties of nature. The starry sky, the sea, and every sight afforded by these wonderful regions, seems still to have the power of elevating his soul from earth. Such a man has a double existence: he may suffer misery, and be overwhelmed by disappointments; yet, when he has retired into himself, he will be like a celestial spirit that has a halo around him, within whose circle no grief or folly ventures.

-Mary Shelley,
'Frankenstein; or, The Modern Prometheus'

19. TREE FROG
To Thy Transformation Be True

Oh, how you've changed. In a glorious celebration of your amphibious nature, you can move from creek to land to tree and back again – without any sign of rust or corrosion in your springs. This **self-driven transformation has expanded your world**. Possibilities and opportunities are opening before you. Yet, still, there is an expectation that **there is more to come**.

You can swim and leap and climb, and this brings you so much joy. It seems a strange suggestion that something is missing – something 'other' that would complete your transition and, at last, have you living happily ever after. And it is oddly fascinating that these suggestions are delivered with an air of benevolence as if **the person most qualified** to know what makes you happy **is not yourself**.

Far, far away from those well-meaning comments and patronising smiles, an amphibious chorus rises with the steam in the moonlight.

The collective mantra is a powerful affirmation that lives within you. **No one knows you as you do**. The only being you change for is yourself. In all your forms, you are whole.

You have matured, changed shape and crossed realms. While you hardly resemble your original form, there are still those who seek to change you entirely: "All it would take is for you to wish hard enough, to be good enough or to meet someone truly fair …" But the charmed idealism they want for you holds no appeal. Why would you relinquish your ability to traverse realms to fit in with a fabled expectation? You may, of course, choose to improve your design. There are other realms to explore, and, one day, you might add wings and fly.

20. NINE-BANDED ARMADILLO

Armoured Compassion

Unperturbed by the low growl of the night machines and manufactured hot air, you plough out under the moonlight. The pleasant countenances of daylight are gone. The faces you pass never quite turn your way or meet your eye. They are the disinterested, the itinerant, the anonymous and the altered, and they warrant no harm or attention. Your purpose lies beyond these hapless wanderers, for now.

You have your own business here, but should you be asked for time or direction, you will readily oblige, for you have both to spare. Your conscientious acceptance of others has opened hearts and healed worlds, and you shall not turn away from **a genuine request for help**. There is a vulnerability in reaching out and in responding. **Acknowledge** the bravery on **all sides**.

There is an easy kindness in your demeanour that extends an invitation to the lost and the lonely. Any light in the dark attracts the waylaid and the waylayers. You are prepared for both. Respect can be granted freely, but your trust is tucked safely beneath your armour. Those who mistake benevolence for weakness, try to trade on sympathy or swindle your attention will meet a stern, dry well. Opportunism is not personal, and neither is your response. You stonewall misdirection or selfishness. **Your resources** are limited and **are to be protected**.

It is no contradiction to be compassionate and guarded. Indeed, it is the softness of your underbelly that warrants your hardened exterior. One warm night does not a summer make, and one act of goodness does not warrant your absolute trust. People show themselves in their consistency. Wear your armour and say no with pride. Those who don't or won't hear your 'no', do not deserve your 'yes'.

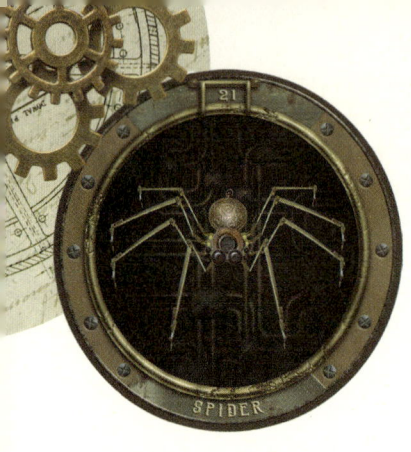

21. SPIDER
The Roar of Distant Wonder

Wide-eyed alert and tiptoe poised, you still your breath so it doesn't affect the fine-tuning of your instruments. The usual thrum of triumph arises from the north while the murmurs of trepidation echo from the south. The motion from the west remains steady and predictable. Yet from the east, an unfamiliar rumble causes unease to stir within you.

Senses activated, you isolate and magnify the strange oscillations, but identifying their source proves tricky. Amidst the interference and mixed messages, you are **look**ing **for a** clear and consistent **sign**al. Until it is identified and classified as non-threatening, you remain vigilant.

This is not your first uncertain horizon. These vibrations could be reminiscent of another time … they could hold a warning that will help you anticipate all that is ahead. So, attention piqued, you keep your senses on point and wait. Even when the vibrations fade, you remain watchful and wonder what it could be long into the night. Until, at last, your body relents into sleep.

Only time will show how justified you were in staying watchful. This time, it was nothing. It could have been something, but if it was, the disturbance underfoot would have been bigger, louder and less elusive. As the web of life spins anew each day, dampen the sensitivity of your equipment. Move the dial from 'high alert' to 'just another average day with little to worry about'. Breathe. You can trust your senses.

22. BILBY
Pause the Fuss

There is much to be told, so much the world does not already know of the circumstances of your arrival. There is still intrigue surrounding your departure! It is only proper to mark your homecoming, to put a proper finish to your fantastic voyage with fanfare, speeches and toasts. Which is why you make your re-entry quietly.

Plunging headlong into unknown and spiralling burrows is all part of the treasure trade. Should one wish **to recoup lost, hidden or abandoned jewels**, one must **go to them**. It is not their business to meet you halfway – not even part of the way. It is always by one's own efforts that a treasure is found.

These ventures have no success guaranteed. Even when a particular gem eludes re-discovery, there is always some passing peril or momentous marvel to regale a dinner party – but not tonight. The time for entertaining eager ears will come. Tonight's treasure is rest.

It's been quite a journey, and there will be questions, celebrations and invitations. So you have crept inside, brewed some tea and run a bath. The ballyhoo can wait a few days (maybe weeks?) until you have welcomed yourself home. You can revisit your story at your leisure. When you are ready to re-engage … oh my, what a tale will be told!

An appreciative listener
is always stimulating.

-Agatha Christie,
'The Mysterious Affair at Styles'

23. HUMBOLDT SQUID
Legends of Bold

In the midnight zone, legends loom large enough to redirect ships and curve a sailor's spine. While the accounts do differ, the similarities suggest there is truth at their core. With matters such as these, imagination is apt to run deep and wild with very little encouragement. It is your task to **sift the strange from the fiction**.

With repeated tellings, blatant myth and hyperbole can garner credulity. Their mundane and curious detail can be intoxicating. You know you have been taken by their charms. But now, armed with the radiant tendrils of eightfold belief, you are set to challenge their veracity.

This is to be an active confrontation. Dive swiftly and take hold of these legends before they can change shape. They will **shift** their **focus** and provide compelling evidence that contradicts and confounds. Set their tales in ink, assess them coldly, make bold erasures **and hold** your corrections **to** the highest standards of **your purpose**.

Do the stories in your midnight zone, the depths of your consciousness, reflect your evolving insight into the noble nature of reality? Challenge the oceanscape of their intention, speech and action. Hold them accountable to you. Crush the falsehoods and cultivate nurturing beliefs so the ships that pass are buoyed by tales of hope and illumination.

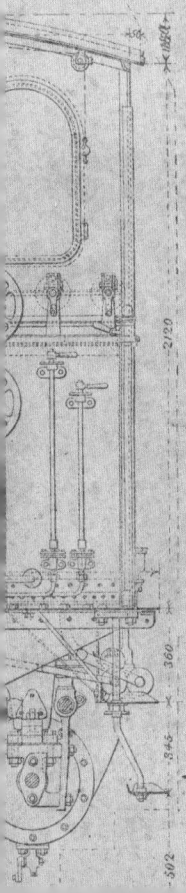

Then it was that there came
into my head the first of the
mad notions that contributed
so much to save our lives.

-Robert Louis Stevenson,
'Treasure Island'

24. HERMIT CRAB
The Soulful Listener

Within your queer and comfortable lodgings, **you have all you need** and more to satisfy your days with musing and romanticism, delight and discovery. Though you do not crave outside company, you don't shun it. And in the event that you find yourself at a banquet or party, you will be remembered for your calm yet lively features and keen fascination for the lives and goings on of the wider world. And thus, the discovery was made.

Others had overlooked or under-assumed your subject for years. Yet, on your first meeting, something glinting in their eye or hinted at in their expression piqued your interest. The conversation that followed, albeit in a crowded space, had the intimacy of lifelong companionship. **Sincere questions, insightful responses and a ready ear** unlocked humble tales of valiance and accomplishment. And then, artfully, with their assent, another ear was added to your circle, and then another, until the room (or select members therein) was held in thrall, exclaiming, "How did we never know this? That's amazing!"

So, while stirring from your shell is a rare occasion, it is not because you are unsociable. Should someone find their way into your morning graces, the conversation could roll long into the afternoon. But as company goes, a freshly printed book, an unexpected chord change or the shifting hues of a cloud-tasselled dawn are just as welcome.

It is, perhaps, inner contentment that fosters your acceptance and interest in others. You would seek to change another being as much as you would alter the colours in a rainbow. And you open your senses to listen to the full spectrum of both. The wallflower, the sea garden and the sunset are like philosopher's wine. You savour it all, feeling the oceanic connections of life in the quiet comfort of your soul.

There is a pleasure in the pathless woods,

There is a rapture on the lonely shore,

There is society where none intrudes,

By the deep Sea, and music in its roar:

I love not Man the less, but Nature more,

From these our interviews, in which I steal

From all I may be, or have been before,

To mingle with the Universe, and feel

What I can ne'er express, yet cannot all conceal.

-Lord Byron,
'Childe Harold's Pilgrimage'

25. SCARAB BEETLE
The Glitter Bug

Oh, **the** night is a **comfort**ing blanket **of** closeness and **anonymity**. Beneath its veil, assured that no prying eyes are near, you venture to your clandestine chambers. Here, you tend to your precious jewels, preserving their faint glimmers and shimmers through your polished care. One day, these treasures will have their time in the sun, their true beauty on show for all to see.

These covert gems are your **private** pleasures. Rubies, sapphires, diamonds and emeralds – skill, passion, **dreams and ambition**, all tucked away from interfering eyes. And from hands that might take and words that might question the value of your hoard.

The glow-worm-like ambience **grow**s as you imagine the opportunities, admiration and security this treasure will bring. But, always, doubt fades **your flame**. In the light of day, your diamonds could be glass, and your rubies stone. What you believe to be valuable may **be** a fool's gold. So, you carefully wrap and hide your gems away, **content to wait** until you are sure of their worth. Until then, you **rehearse for excellence** in shadows and solitude.

Your umbral adventures reveal fantasy and truth. The jewels you hide are keys to your hopes and talents. Bring them to light one by one. Begin with the smallest if you wish. Their many facets were unremarkable in the darkness. Out in the sun, you will see their worth was unfairly assessed. They are greater prizes than you realise.

Few of us now have seen the stars as folk saw them then—our cities and towns cast too much light on the night—but, from the village of Wall, the stars were laid out like worlds or like ideas, uncountable as the trees in forest or the leaves on a tree.

-Neil Gaiman,
'Stardust'

26. DUMBO OCTOPUS

Almost Fathomless

This is not a mere retreat into emptiness but a full-breathed transition into the extreme tranquillity of a deeper realm. You have not withdrawn from life, not even for a moment. Nay, you have entered the abyssal heart of existence itself. Within the lush quiet and bustling serenity, it may be tempting to follow the echoes of the past forever. Instead, you **go deeper**.

The natural and the supernatural stir all around you. In a feat of oceanic wonder, there is no separation between them. The absurd, the rational and the fantastical are co-existing companions, drifting and growing and merging in and out of each other's tenuous outlines. You are aware of their shifting shapes, but they do not tempt you as they have before, and you sink further, ever further.

Navigating these depths requires inspired mechanisms. Umbrellaing expansion, parachuting buoyancy and pinpoint containment help you drift above the sunken city of your final below. There are Heracleion statues, nests of discarded sea nets and newly nestled relics thrown overboard or lost to the waves in the world far above. You marvel at the monoliths, untangle pearls from the nets, **find treasure in debris and shift your anchor**.

The abyssal realms are almost fathomless. When you sink below drifting distractions and sublime sirens, you will finally reach its base. Nothing can hurt you here, so you can explore without fear. This netherworld is couched in sands of love and emotion and sways the current and flow of all that floats above. You are free to move the pieces of this landscape, to release hooks and untangle threads. Myth lives as reality in the bosom of the abyss – place your anchor with the daring care of an artful explorer and see your world re-ravel.

27. LONG-EARED OWL
Wearing Midnight's Knell

The night rolls open like a reluctant tapestry. Expectant breaths are held, hopeful wishes made and fingers crossed in fervour, but the dye has long been cast. The pattern was decided on the loom. As a friend to time, tested and true, you know the weave of this tale. And as a friend to wisdom, tested and new, you watch and wait, prepared for all eyes to turn to you.

The faces and places change, but all this has happened before. You have told the tales, gifted the counsel and knelled the warnings, but there will always be those compelled to live the roles and learn the lessons for themselves. You **respect their choice** and their unwillingness to sacrifice direct experience for the passive acceptance of another's wisdom.

The familiar weave is an ochraceous blend tinted with shades of grey. Part of you hopes that the mechanisms of fate will be defied, and the tale will take a surprising tack. Though outwardly unmoved, you take the sympathetic journey, revisiting every flutter or emotion as if it were your first time here. When the deeds are done and the tale unspun, you will **be there with** midnight **comfort**.

Harder than living our own heartaches is watching others, especially those we love, move through their own hardships. The harbinger ignored is the one that proves true and grows trusted. And here, in this vulnerable space, the most valuable lessons are grown. There is no scolding, "I told you so," only welcoming wings of, "I am here for you, I understand you, I love you."

28. CLAWED LOBSTER

Empowered Attachment

Is it not inevitable that you should, at least on occasion, do your utmost to avoid, deny and run from the inevitable? Change can be unpleasant and scary. Outcomes can be uncertain. So, you hold tight and declare that everything is fine just as it is. Or good enough. Or not so bad. Or you cling to the hope things will come good. However, there is always a part of you that sees and knows what must happen.

Temperatures can rise so slowly. It's possible not to notice the little ways you are accommodating discomfort. There can be a quiet (barely detectable) erosion of autonomy, vision or motivation, but there is a part of **you** that **cannot be diminished**. The part that learns and expands and pushes against the constraints of 'fine'. When you attach to less than, it **reach**es **for something** more, something **truer to you**.

The discomfort of remaining in your current shell will become bigger than the perceived discomfort that change could bring. Fighting the inevitable can take a lot of energy. By the time you are ready to welcome the new, you may feel weary and vulnerable and ill-prepared to direct your course with confidence. You have long since prepared for this moment and grown more than you realise.

Yes, you will be vulnerable for a time. The very fortress of your identity may have been levelled. Retreat as needed. Take comfort in rest and nurturing company. Accept support. Be informed. Actively choose the values and freedoms your expanded self wants to attach to. When the energy spent fighting against your dreams (against yourself) is redirected, it is multiplied. You will be reinvigorated and courageously naked in your pursuit of something better. You will emerge more capable, more powerful and more content with yourself.

29. BUTTERFLY
Salvaged Beauty

To one side, the lake, to the other verdant hills, the port in the middle, your heart stills. Above it all, you rise and sail on the breath that whispers a cautious tale. **History can repeat itself** and often does so in patterns and lilts that colour decisions and taunt expectations. In a feat of ingenuity, you shaped wings from a legacy of wheels and water and taught yourself to **fly** above and **beyond**.

The tragedy, scandal and heroic ghosts of other times and places could weigh upon your heart and your hope. But the fortunes of the past are not your curses to bear. Though you have taken the lessons and blessings and built from them with pride, **the chronicles** that truly interest you are **not yet written**.

The stories of your ancestors are like postcards from faraway places. They don't define you, but they can **inspire you**. Traditions that once fostered connection may now seem like a duty paid to a lost world.

You are not here as an echo of the past but as a herald of the future.

The mechanisms put in motion in the past can be pulled apart and remodelled to meet modernity. Cogs can turn the hands of time or a paddlewheel, and now you can fashion them to create your own legacy. Respect your past through new conventions of innovation, freedom and actualisation.

V: There are two bodies - the rudimental and the complete; corresponding with the two conditions of the worm and the butterfly. What we call "death," is but the painful metamorphosis. Our present incarnation is progressive, preparatory, temporary. Our future is perfected, ultimate, immortal. The ultimate life is the full design.

P: But of the worm's metamorphosis we are palpably cognizant.

V: We, certainly - but not the worm. The matter of which our rudimental body is composed, is within the ken of the organs of that body; or, more distinctly, our rudimental organs are adapted to the matter of which is formed the rudimental body; but not to that of which the ultimate is composed. The ultimate body thus escapes our rudimental senses, and we perceive only the shell which falls, in decaying, from the inner form; not that inner form itself; but this inner form, as well as the shell, is appreciable by those who have already acquired the ultimate life.

-Edgar Allan Poe,
'Mesmeric Revelation'.
Dialogue between mesmerist (P) and patient in trance (V)

30. PANGOLIN
Elusive Destination

And at the top of the world, at what you thought was as far as there was to go, there is another height to climb. **You have come so far** on your many-treasured journey. This was to be your moment of completion, your place of repose. But how can you rest when just ahead there is a better view, cleaner air and brighter stars? One more ascent, and surely, you'll be there.

The fire in your dragon's heart is not yet quenched, and tomorrow calls with promises and reassurances. Just beyond the sunrise or the next full moon is all you have strived for, maybe even more. How sweet it will be to add this sparkling **new triumph** to your tales. This **will** be the chapter that **makes the journey** feel **whole**.

You continue forwards, ever forward. Until … you pause to adjust your footing, your grip or your stance, and **a spark on the horizon** draws your eye. You've been so keenly focussed on the road ahead, but now you are looking back over the long road you have travelled. That distant light **shines from your past**, where friends, family and memories live on.

You've come a long way – far further than you had planned. When you began, you dreamed of your jubilant return. Faces would light up at your success. There would be books to write, youth to inspire and glory to hold. And now, though you have nothing left to prove, you are compelled by the road ahead. Perhaps you may never return, but in taking in the true wonder of just how far you have come, you can afford yourself some rest. You are already whole.

And, sure enough, it was a dragon—a great, shining, winged, scaly, clawy, big-mouthed dragon—made of pure ice. It must have gone to sleep curled around the hole where the warm steam used to come up from the middle of the earth, and then when the earth got colder, and the column of steam froze and was turned into the North Pole, the dragon must have got frozen in his sleep—frozen too hard to move—and there he stayed. And though he was very terrible he was very beautiful too.

-E. Nesbit,
'The Book of Dragons'

31. STONE CRAB
Testing the Mettle

Oh, substantive destiny! The entire matter is an intricate labyrinth of enigma and majesty, my dear friend. The potential held within its puzzling nature is undoubtedly great, yet the solutions remain elusive. Sorting the facts from the spurious requires a combination of youthful enthusiasm and mature methodology. Though some may scoff at the quest, branding it a fool's errand, remember that today's fool is often tomorrow's visionary. Therefore, it is **a pursuit well worth time and effort**.

You have taken to sorting your stones not by size, hue or density but by meaning and application. They are lifted, grasped, weighed, squeezed and pried to reveal their unbreakable cores but catalogued under labels such as helpful, inconsequential, nurturing, discouraging, remarkable and undecided.

You've found that it doesn't matter how often you poke and prod at a truth, it will remain solid. And a tiny grain of untarnished wisdom may hold the greatest benefits. The conceptual and interpretable can be the glue that binds and the **honey** that **sweetens** and allows the benefits of **a truth** to be carried and absorbed. The sum of the whole doesn't equal the sum of the parts.

Prying the truth from a situation isn't always as important as recognising its meaning. Myth, suggestion and feeling can shape the future as much, or more, than a sharply defined fact. In the end, truth can wane and rise. So, collect your stones, test their mettle, and draw from your catalogue to substantiate your destiny with kindness, compassion and gracious understanding.

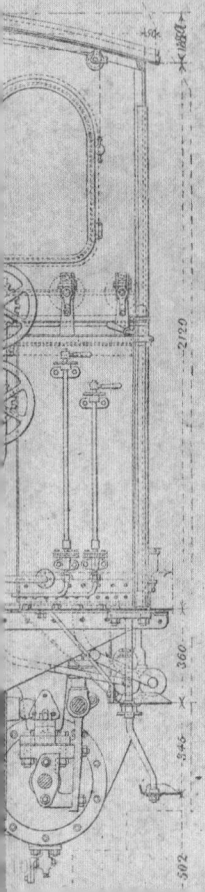

"But this was not a method, it was an idea, that might lead to a method by which it would be possible, without changing any other property of matter—except, in some instances colours—to lower the refractive index of a substance, solid or liquid, to that of air – so far as all practical purposes are concerned."

"Phew!" said Kemp. "That's odd! But still, I don't see quite … I can understand that thereby you could spoil a valuable stone, but personal invisibility is a far cry."

-H.G. Wells,
'The Invisible Man: A Grotesque Romance'

32. GIANT ISOPOD
The Lore of the Deep

The pressure in the midnight zone is that of one hundred atmospheres. The weight of the ocean does not crush or compact those that dwell here. Rather, it stimulates the profound power of the ancestors and the behemoth wizened by ancient tides. You move and feel with this power, a giant of this time and place, strong in life and fierce in love.

Not all who happen here have learned to activate the lore of the deep. It's easy to remember back to when you were new to these depths – the desire to find cover, thinking you would be overwhelmed by the great heaviness above you. Perhaps it would be easier to **forget the doubt** and the panic and the fear, but it all comes flooding back through the eyes of the newcomers you meet. They stir memories and compassion and gratitude.

In the memories, you relive vulnerability. Not just your own but of all who came before and those who will follow. Compassion arises for who you were, all you have become, all who came before and all who will follow. You are awash with gratitude for those who offered an easy benevolence so that you may show kindness now that will, in turn, be passed to others. **The weight** above **cannot compare to the supports, connections and inner resources you have** found in the deep.

This strange, deep place is home to mysterious, deep creatures. They think and feel deep. Whatever the source of the pressure, (whatever the magnitude of salty droplets represents) the response springs from an innate convergent design. It reminds us, slowly, gently and surely, that together and alone, we are giants. The hours breathe faint and low as you cross the midnight zone. You will emerge from the weight of this world, but your strengths, compassions, gratitudes and wisdoms live on, as part of you, always.

33. SEAHORSE
A Chaotic Call to Calm

A stray beam of daylight penetrated the shroud of steam and flotsam to illuminate this very spot. It called to you, beckoning you from your place of shelter, out into open space and unbridled currents. And now here you are, bewildered, and vulnerable, and wondering what path lies ahead. Yet **do not be discouraged**, for you possess the luxury of ponderment. The same siren of light that coaxed you from your comfort has also unveiled an unyielding safehold, a sanctuary amidst the tumultuous seas.

It's not that you didn't listen to the tales of foreboding. Nor that you didn't heed them. In this instance, the allure was too much. Its haunting, hopeful charms lullabied caution and made drunk your desires. The decision to lose yourself to the tides was not one of heart or mind or soul. It was answering to a primal yearning awakened and enlivened by that simple, penetrating show of light.

Later, you can explore the questions of why you were called and why you responded. For now, **hold** tight **to what you know**, who you know yourself to be and wait. Calm will come. You cannot hurry its arrival, but you can prepare for it. Anchor yourself to the unmoveable–chain yourself to it!–**and preserve your energy**. There's no need to feel brave, ashamed, guilty, defeated, bewildered, hopeless, sad, belligerent, alone, sorry or regretful. And there's no need not to. Whatever **feelings come and go** with the swirling tide are okay. **Focus on the unchanging** self and let them pass.

As the distant echoes of reproach gradually fade, you regain your composure and vigour and understand that you are okay. The supports you cling to will not let you down – not now, not ever. This realisation hushes your trepidation and rekindles your conviction, enabling you to open your eyes to the marvels of your surroundings and acknowledge all you risked reaching this point. When the calm comes, you shall discern your destination with clarity. Will you choose ease, pandemonium or something between?

34. GARDEN SNAIL
Getting to the Start

Today, the great and unexplored turbine of truth shall remain both great and unexplored. But fret not, for you will trek through its very heart and map its endless wonders. With your equipment at the ready and meticulous plans in place, **you will never be more prepared** for this epic endeavour. All you need to do is **begin**. The turbine of truth will still be there tomorrow. So, what is the hurry?

The undertaking before you is bold. Once you begin, there may be no turning back, so you want to ensure nothing has been forgotten or overlooked. You want to consider every possibility. And this is the crux of your delay. How can you prepare for every conceivable outcome when you are unsure of what to expect?

You have contingency supplies, routes and power sources. But what if you become lost, have miscalculated or move too slow? You can pack an extra compass, verify your math and determine your ideal pace, yet there is always another quandary to answer, another worry to quell. All the while, a more significant question is growing: what if you never embark?

Thank the part of you that wants to keep you safe by trying to anticipate all eventualities. Thank it for its love and for striving to protect you. Thank it for alerting you to possible dangers and disappointments. Be grateful for its care and concern, and then acknowledge that there will be trials ahead. Reassure yourself–all of yourself–that you are ready for them. You are an adventurer, and the truth is out there, waiting for you. Set forth and begin!

"'Will you walk a little faster?' said a whiting to a snail.

"There's a porpoise close behind us, and he's treading on my tail.

See how eagerly the lobsters and the turtles all advance!

They are waiting on the shingle - will you come and join the dance?

Will you, won't you, will you, won't you, will you join the dance?

Will you, won't you, will you, won't you, won't you join the dance?

"You can really have no notion how delightful it will be

When they take us up and throw us, with the lobsters, out to sea!"

But the snail replied "Too far, too far!" and gave a look askance -

Said he thanked the whiting kindly, but he would not join the dance.

Would not, could not, would not, could not, would not join the dance.

Would not, could not, would not, could not, could not join the dance.

"What matters it how far we go?" his scaly friend replied.

"There is another shore, you know, upon the other side.

The further off from England the nearer is to France –

Then turn not pale, beloved snail, but come and join the dance.

Will you, won't you, will you, won't you, will you join the dance?

Will you, won't you, will you, won't you, won't you join the dance?"

-Lewis Carroll,
'Alice's Adventures in Wonderland'

35. AXOLOTL
Sagacious Frivolity

With its feathered gills and dances of love, you have embraced and re-embraced the wonders and delights of the aquatic lifestyle many times over. And should there be another battle or misadventure, you will **call on your** otherworldly **ability to** regenerate and **rebuild** to the same water-loving, youth-inspired, joy-honouring design. There will be no scars or wounds worn on your sleeves – no visible testimony to the conflict, pain or loss endured. Life is, indeed, too short.

Difficulties, troubles and hardships (circumstances you had no agency over) tried to steal or diminish your days of lazy leisure and carefree pleasure. But you did not and will not relinquish your **claim to happiness and** will forever **honour your** divine **inner youth**. Yes, there are warriors who wear their battle marks with pride. Yes, there are survivors who roar their might into protection for the now vulnerable. And yes, there are those who nod to your folly and see it not as immaturity but as a defiant affirmation that the pains of life have no hold on your soul. You are youthful, aged and wizened, and you lend your fool's treasure to the warrior, the survivor, the supporter and the vulnerable. For you, it is a laugh, a skip and **a pocket of silliness** that buoys hope and **restores light** in the world.

On this idle afternoon, there are plans for frivolous frivolity and profound elevation, and everyone is welcome. The only condition is that they are ready and willing to **be open to** a splash of fun. And if joy doesn't come for them today, that's okay. Osmosis will do its part. In this pond of play, make-believe rules begin to dissolve and disappear – without any harmful consequences! When the **joy** seeps in, it is childishly, delightfully good.

Should a flippant quip or a cheery pun rise above the rubble of chaos, trouble or heartache, it is not because you aren't taking things seriously. It is because you know that life is precious and that hope is energised by laughter and goodwill. The smile you offer is not born of optimism but from the hard-won knowledge that people and circumstances can come in all shapes and kindness. Some will see a fool, others a sage. And in both countenances, there is freedom.

36. LONG-HORNED BEETLE

A Circle of Feeling

A wrinkle in the leaves, a crinkle in the wind, a twinkle falling through the canopy … the morning pours through your senses like syrup and sawdust. The scene is simple, intoxicating, promising and terrifying. Probabilities and possibilities are heightened with the immediacy of the day, and there comes the overwhelming awareness that in an instant, so subtly unlike any other, **anything can happen**.

Ah … with a purposeful pause, you **ease into** the magic of **the moment and** stretch your antennae over your awareness zone. The leaf dust underfoot connects you with the heart of the earth, and time is comforted by its deep and steady beat. Here, now, in your circle of feeling, the world slows, and you can take in its signals at your own pace.

Delicately, you sift through the sights, smells and symphony of your surroundings. There is a warning here not to be missed. You felt its urgency tugging at the hem of your consciousness, and now, in your personal sphere of tranquillity, you give it space. Without hurry, competition or panic, you see it is a warning to **welcome** – alerting you to **revelation**, gratitude, miracle and opportunity.

On the forest floor, with life towering above and rustling below, the output of the world can be overwhelming. Luckily, you don't need to take on or take in the whole world. Bring your awareness close to create a circle of feeling where you are a maven of time and sensation. Here you can survey all you sense at your own pace. The now is extended, foreboding becomes foresight, and you have the opportunity and wherewithal to respond with purposeful calm.

37. ORANDA GOLDFISH
Real World Imaginings

Another day bubbles with daydreams and golden linings and nothing that has to be done. Perhaps you'll do a little more on that filigree you've been fussing over in splashes and spurts. It's ever so lovely, and you'll see whether the finishing touches are ready to reveal themselves when you swim by. If not, there are other whims and projects to **potter and ponder** and drift between.

Conversations and inspirations swim through your mind in a mix of memory and things yet to be. It's fun to play and replay scenes with different characters and dialogues. They could all rhyme in verse or move in reverse and have their fins painted yellow. Oh, what an interesting time that would be. You might paint it now or just look at some clouds …

In the end, things get done in the way that they will. Not the way that the outer world prescribes them to be. All **your creations** already exist and **wait to be found**. There is no hurrying their discovery. Birthing ideas and artistry may not look like labour. They say the real world runs on timetables, not dreams. But it is their world that is make-believe.

You can flit and flourish in a space of your own creation where imagination rules. Here, you are free to flow into ways of doing and being that work for you. Those who visit have a real experience of love and beauty and peace. They return to their worlds and see the reality it lacks. You are not alone in your pond. You are looked after and protected. This is not to keep you safe from the real world but so you can keep the real world of dreams and imaginings safe and accessible to all.

She walked slowly round the deck, gazing to right and left and above, incapable for the moment either of thought or speech, but only of dumb wonder, mingled with a dim sense of overwhelming awe. Presently she craned her neck backwards and looked straight up to the zenith. A huge silver crescent, supporting, as it were, a dim greenish-coloured body in its arms, stretched overhead across nearly a sixth of the heavens.

Then Redgrave came to her side, took her in his arms, lifted her as if she had been a little child, and laid her in a long, low deck-chair, so that she could look at it without inconvenience.

The splendid crescent seemed to be growing visibly bigger, and as she lay there in a trance of wonder and admiration she saw point after point of dazzling white light flash out in the dark portions, and then begin to send out rays as though they were gigantic volcanoes in full eruption, and were pouring torrents of living fire from their blazing craters.

"Sunrise on the Moon!" said Redgrave, who had stretched himself on another chair beside her. "A glorious sight, isn't it? But nothing to what we shall see to-morrow morning – only there doesn't happen to be any morning just about here."

"Yes," she said dreamily, "glorious, isn't it? That and all the stars – but I can't think anything yet, Lenox, it's all too mighty and too marvellous. It doesn't seem as though human eyes were meant to look upon things like this."

-George Griffith,
'A Honeymoon in Space'

38. HORSESHOE CRAB

The Probability Engine

It was **a surprise**, even to you, that the copper-based elements of your design would respond to the tides and the moon. As their fullness approaches, the engine gently hums to life. It is fitting that, ultimately, such a machine should be a product of luck. The resourceful wrangling together of substitutes, like a pumice-stone core and a saw-toothed rudder, created something beyond the sum of the parts.

It was not luck, but trial and curiosity that unlocked what it could do. And now, as the peak moment approaches, you enter your goal, irrelevant data is cut free, and likelihood filters through the heart of the machine. The eight legs adjust, and your course is set. It would be easy to miss the magic at work because there is no guaranteed outcome. However, you have discovered that success often comes down to an incremental increase in probability.

Adjusting your view, intention, speech, thinking, focus, company, efforts and input by a few notches here and there can edge you ever closer to success. But that **is not the whole story**! The probability engine is so effective because it does not deal with absolutes and singularities. Ask a question, and it will give you a list of jobs to apply for, people to date or chances to take. And you are to **increase your odds** by applying for, meeting or **try**ing **them all**!

Fate is on your side. Give it a boost by adjusting your approach and broadening your prospects. Narrow your options to handfuls of possibilities that most appeal to you. Every thought, attempt, connection and reflection draws success closer. It is just a matter of time before one of the many ways you apply yourself to your dream turns the probable into the actual.

39. SHOEBILL STORK

Talking the Walk

The broad disc of day splashes at the horizon, washing it anew with bursts of rose and gold. At this gentle time, the heat is quiet, comforting and enlivening. The steam's sibilance is not yet lost to the clutter and cloud of the rushing hours. You wade into the world's **awaken**ing with long, patient strides and the best of company – **your** fresh, open, imaginative **mind**.

There are two parts at play here. There is the part of you that is absorbed in the elements of the morning, in awe of the flow of the dawn, unable and uninterested in slowing its rising colours or warming glow. And there is the 'you' that is immersed in the future. Here, they meet and talk and ponder and shake off the things that cannot be changed and walk through the many ways to make the changes that can (and will) be made.

You talk your walk and walk your talk, **in a supportive dialogue** between observer and participant. The meeting of theory and application, acceptance and intention, stillness and activity magnifies the wisdom and insights of both parts. Later, your calm, cool and sharp responses will seem and feel instinctive and unprepared. Yet, they are charged with confidence and metered out **with big-picture understanding**.

In the soft glow of the rose dawn, action is ritual and words are incantation. Talk your emboldened walk and walk your inspired talk, in solitude and gratitude. With the sacred magic of self-awareness, your words and actions will become natural expressions of your values, intentions and purpose. You will be all that is needed in each moment, be it still and patient or quick acting and fierce. Talk to and know thyself and trust the tick and tock of your walk will rise to the chime of every occasion.

40. BOXFISH
The Pandora Effect

Rusted, encrusted, wrapped in chains, locked and abandoned on the reef – that's how you found it. And that's how it could stay. Someone went to a lot of trouble to bring the box to this place and hide it amongst the coral. They must have had **a good** reason to **secret** it away. They must have been concerned it was not hidden well enough. A caution etched to stand the tests of time can be clearly read: "Danger. Do not open. Do not touch."

This box and its contents are none of your business. There could be terrible things inside that you will never be able to unsee or unknow. Ignoring the obvious signs could have dire consequences. Against all the common sense that tells you to **leave well enough alone**, curiosity whispers, "Let's have one little look. What could possibly go wrong?"

This box is asking to be noticed, begging to be unlocked. If it wasn't so intriguing, the warning not so foreboding, you could have swum on by. Its forbidden, unpredictable nature is a tantalising siren's song and your better judgement wavers in its thrall. You could come to regret what happens next, but if you don't open that box, you will be left wondering forever. Curiosity will win—has won—but you do not yet know whether its prize will be treasure or tragedy, empowerment or peril.

You pause and prepare for whatever may come next, and it strikes you that you recognise this feeling. The suspense, the unknowing, the intrigue, the danger, the realisation that the risk will be worth the discovery. You have your own secrets locked away. You know they will one day be released, that your curious drive to understand, heal and be whole will triumph over caution and fear. Perhaps it is time to take a peek?

ONE-MINUTE MESSAGES

1. **Galago:** Putting something aside to free up time, energy or progress. Disregarding the usual method and fast-tracking progress. Swinging back to an interest, a responsibility or a pleasure. A rekindled love or hobby.

2. **Carpenter Bee:** Emerging with renewed energy and enthusiasm. Responding to a challenge or difficult personality with poise, presence and detachment. A solo pursuit or task requires consistent effort (small actions often).

3. **Anglerfish:** Assess a new acquaintance or colleague with a wary eye. A red flag is precisely what it seems. Acknowledge and assess coping strategies – are they helping or hindering? A situation requires unusual knowledge.

4. **Praying Mantis:** Playing the long game with patience and purpose. Being content to be overlooked until all the pieces are lined up and ready for action. Encouragement and support from everyday allies.

5. **Meerkat:** Benefitting from an institutional or authoritative system or structure for the greater good. A crafty means to

an end. Alternative thinking and communities. Family–those recognised as family–sticking together for fun and prosperity.

6. **Nautilus:** A pattern or opportunity resurfaces. Moving with instinct and enlightenment: trust the feelings, guide the actions. Compartmentalising. Attending to one emotion, task or situation at a time. A deeper understanding improves outcomes.

7. **House Wren:** Activity, multi-tasking and busyness. Satisfaction in completing minor tasks and kicking small goals. Routine, planning and to-do lists create momentum, focus and much-needed relaxation time. Scheduling and protecting periods of rest.

8. **Dragonfly:** Warming to an idea, new project or relationship. Acknowledging that genius takes time. Giving plans, insights, abilities and opinions time to mature. Adapting your approach to your circumstance.

9. **Puffer Fish:** Seeing, believing and nurturing the vulnerable. Providing an actual or energetic safe haven. Calm and fierce protective instincts – perhaps being surprised by them. Stepping in to de-escalate or de-fuse an issue.

10. **Wombat:** A surge of innovation and realisation. Putting one's mind to a riddle or problem and staying with it for a surprising outcome. Transforming 'good enough' into 'amazing' with study, focus and time.

11. **Cicada:** Admitting your goals and making your intentions known. Expanding networks. Saying yes to invites and opportunities and turning up ready to make connections. Daring to be openly enthusiastic about transforming a dream into reality. Seeking and accepting help.

12. **Chameleon:** Feeling uncertain of who one is, was and may become in a new situation. Blending in for now. Actively transforming disappointment into a golden moment. Rewriting personal myths. Seeing triumph in tragedy.

13. **Sea Jellies:** Planning and foresight go unappreciated. Efficiency and proven methodology are met with a bigger workload. Learning to say no to extra tasks. Support from those who know the effort it takes to make the complex seem simple.

14. **Little Brown Bat:** Engaging with a chaotic character is ill-advised. The shock that follows a disruptive event or behaviour. Resolving an issue by disengaging from it. A sense of self provides anchoring calm within a storm.

15. **House Fly:** The beginnings of a rumour. Disrupting the chain of gossip. Exaggerated claims or half-truths. Checking references and sourcing testimonies. The pieces of a story fall into place in unexpected ways.

16. **Tortoise:** Wisdom beyond experience or time. Foundational dreams or plans. An innate understanding of an issue or an easily picked-up skill. Sharing intimate stories of challenge, heartache and triumph. Deep and lasting connections.

17. **Koala:** Revisiting a troubling event with fresh information or new tools of understanding. Intense re-evaluation and self-analysis. A matter-of-fact approach to an emotional challenge. Logic as a coping strategy. Detached awareness could be mistaken for disinterest.

18. **Spanner Crab:** Throwing a spanner in the works – for good! Seeing possibility in the 'broken'. An unusual experience or upbringing that bears unusual abilities and wisdom. Niche ideas and specialisation. A curious issue requires a quirky approach.

19. **Tree Frog:** Internal transformation transcends external expectation. A leap in consciousness or status that defies myth and consensus. Personal change causes discomfort to another. Taking pride in the journey so far. Owning all that is to come.

20. **Nine-Banded Armadillo:** A compassionate and well-guarded heart. Ensuring well-meant help is not a hindrance. Being kind, not foolish. Distinguishing between the vulnerable and the devious. Giving by choice. Setting and protecting boundaries as an act of love.

21. **Spider:** A reminder of a personality, pattern or event that sparks hyper-awareness and worry for the future. Striving to avoid the repeat of a challenging situation that was beyond your control (and is unlikely to reoccur). Mapping out the journey from panic to peace.

22. **Bilby:** Quietly savouring success or satisfaction. Rest and re-centring at the end of a journey, process or task. Celebrating positive outcomes in solitude or with a select group. Enjoying social interaction on one's own terms.

23. **Humboldt Squid:** Record-keeping, diarising and journalling. A deliberate stirring of the waters tests self-belief and perception. A morsel of truth is inflated and distorted to disempower. Reaffirming facts, feelings and identity.

24. **Hermit Crab:** A trusted ear creates a safe space. Happiness in one's own company and interests is an invitation to like souls.

Gratitude and fascination for individual expression. Attentive listening and active interest lead to gentle and mutual sharing.

25. **Scarab Beetle:** Fantasies about what could be. Untapped potential feeds discontent. Fortifying one's comfort zone ... then stretching its boundaries. Attempting or revealing one new skill. Volunteering a solution, a kindness or a helping hand creates shining moments.

26. **Dumbo Octopus:** Addressing a deep-seated issue at its core. Courageously confronting challenging memories, self-beliefs and perceptions. Exploring sadness, worry, doubt, fear, anger or other tricky emotions openly and honestly. Wilfully resetting foundations.

27. **Long-Eared Owl:** Ignored advice deepens trust and first-hand wisdom. Watching a repeating pattern unfold. Compassionate listening as aftercare. Relating to another's heartache. Being gentler with one's past and present selves.

28. **Clawed Lobster:** Discomfort drives a scary but necessary change. Vulnerability is temporary. An all-encompassing task or shift. Attaching to people, places and opportunities that invite wellness, pleasure and healthy excitement.

29. **Butterfly:** Repurposing familial stories, legacies, traditions or skills. Respecting the past by living boldly and proudly in the present. Breaking free of ancestral curses to esteem or identity. Setting a new convention of setting new conventions.

30. **Pangolin:** Forward focus. Feeling that happiness is with the next accomplishment. A pause in progress. Acknowledging the journey and its influence on the 'who, why and what' of dreams. Satisfaction, contentment, wholeness and rest – finally.

31. **Stone Crab:** Cataloguing experiences and information based on their teachings. The message is in the packaging – is it helpful, compassionate and future building? Confronting a tough (and supposed) truth with intention, methodology and objectivity.

32. **Giant Isopod:** Core strengths are activated, embraced and utilised. Innate resourcefulness, know-how and persistence arise and surprise. A pressure that won't lift but can be left behind. Kind deeds and gratitude lighten a load – for one and for all.

33. **Seahorse:** Bowing to temptation with consequence. An uncharacteristic compulsion that circumvents common sense. If something seems too good to be true, talk about it. Holding tight to values, identity, friendships and supports. Plotting a return to tranquillity.

34. **Garden Snail:** Putting off until tomorrow what could already be done. Fear of failure becomes a failure to start. The preamble to beginning something new. Ever-expanding checklists, preparations and contingencies – never feeling ready while being over-prepared!

35. **Axolotl:** Youthful or childlike manner or appearance. An outward flippancy or immaturity as part of a quietly responsible, diligent and caring nature. The gift of play. Refusing to let stress or heartache get in the way of a good time.

36. **Long-Horned Beetle:** High sensitivity. Mindfulness and meditation as a remedy for panic or overwhelm. A warning received calmly is a welcome foresight. Withdrawing attention from the wider world to focus on this moment, this here, this now.

37. **Oranda Goldfish:** Creativity is a real job. Flitting from one inspiration to another. Imagination as power. Rehearsing, replaying or rewriting past or future scenarios for healing. Accepting support while following a dream. Having an artistic talent recognised.

38. **Horseshoe Crab:** Luck is boosted with a little extra effort, thought, connection and interest. Narrowing in on a dream by

broadening the ways to get there. Seeing 'almost' and 'nearly' as part of the process. Looking not for definite outcomes but increased probability.

39. Shoebill Stork: Robust inner dialogue. Active meditation. Aligning intention and instinct. A careful, detailed response arises from big-picture vision and understanding. Supportive self-talk as an agent of change and manifestation. Acting on impulse – with confidence.

40. Boxfish: A battle between curiosity and common sense. Choosing external drama over self-exploration. The suspense between deciding and acting – making it last. A safe choice with predictable results is unappealing – but why? The need for something different (anything different) could be better directed.

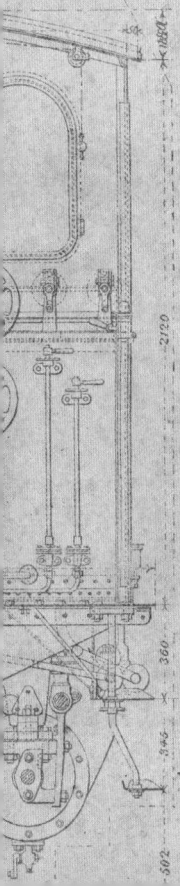

Dear Traveller,

May the winds of fortune be at your back as you embark on new adventures filled with fascinating machines and mysterious lands. Yours is the bravery and boldness that only a true dreamer could possess. May your spirit of invention continue to inspire and rise higher.

Sail time on your airship, descend into lost caverns, speak to other realms and breathe your legend into being. Incredible discoveries await you. We eagerly savour the moments until your return, when we will share in your exploits and celebrate all that is to come. Farewell, for now, dear friend. Our world is richer for knowing you.

The Zoologica

ABOUT THE AUTHOR

Leela J. Williams grew up with stories of her grandmother 'knowing' what was happening with family and friends on the other side of the world. Spiritual connection was a manifestation of love, and it seemed natural to share dreams and secret worlds with her sister. When, as teens, their sensitivities heightened, it further fuelled Leela's fascination with the unseen, and she delved deeper into music, philosophy and metaphysics.

In 2000, Leela's love of books, words, magic and remarkable people melded when she entered the realm of spiritual publishing. She founded The Spirit Guide in 2002, published *Spheres* and *Spellcraft* magazines and co-founded *The Psychics Directory* with the Australian Psychics Association. Leela's contributions to the spiritual field were recognised with a Psychic of the Year Award for Queensland in 2004, a Psychic Ambassador Award in 2013 and the Simon Turnbull Award in 2016. She served as the media spokesperson for the International Psychics Association and had a regular spot on radio for over ten years.

Avidly curious, Leela continues to explore philosophy, mythology and spiritual connection. Her creativity, deep thinking and quirky view of the world have made her a sought-after editor and mentor. She lives in Brisbane, Australia, with her four children and an ever-growing collection of books, oracles, tarot cards and musical instruments.

Leela has co-written or contributed to *Sacred Earth Oracle, Peace Oracle, Precious Gems Oracle, Portraits of Innocence, Kahlil Gibran's The Prophet: An Oracle Card Set, Ancestor Spirit Oracle Cards, Oracle of the Wylder Ones*, and more.

Waves of sincere gratitude extend from my dancing heart to Maxine for trusting me to give voice to her marvellous creations, to Sunshine for her enthusiasm for the steampunk vision throughout the layout and design, and to Toni and Martine for making this, and so many more dreams than this one, come true.

To Rebecca, my sister, here's another dime in the jukebox, baby! It's playing a song of resourcefulness, resilience, invention, companionship, and the radical rewiring of destiny. You know all the moves! So come and take a lime and dance with me.

Leela

ABOUT THE ARTIST

Maxine Gadd has been creating art since early childhood. She uses traditional and digital mediums.

Maxine Gadd Creations is where art and craft come together. For over 20 years, Maxine has been creating beautiful and unique artworks focusing on fantastical creatures. Maxine's art book *Fairies and Other Fantastical Folk* was a bestseller and sold over 45,000 copies.

Now, Maxine is offering her beautiful artwork in the form of cross-stitch charts, diamond paintings and oracle cards. Children's and art books are in progress and will be available on Amazon Books. Whether you're looking for a new art project to spend time on or a way to decorate your home, Maxine Gadd Creations has something for everyone.

www.maxinegaddcreations.com

Discover more treasures from Maxine Gadd's Zoologica at
www.SteampunkZoologica.com

More from Blue Angel Publishing®

PRECIOUS GEMS ORACLE

Maxine Gadd
Inspired verse and divinatory meanings by Leela J. Williams

Welcome to an exquisite, delicate and powerful realm where the magic and wisdom of gemstones come to life. Discover the face of Amethyst, look Emerald in the eye, and delight in the reflective splendour of Moonstone personified. Renowned and beloved artist, Maxine Gadd has fused the wonder of her Imaginarium with the world of gemstones to create an oracle that flawlessly unites practical, earth-based guidance with blessings and higher knowledge.

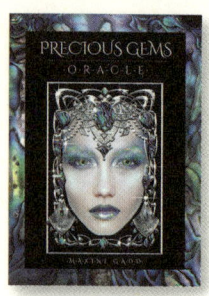

40 cards + 100-page guidebook
packaged in a hardcover box.
ISBN: 978-1-925538-51-9

More from Blue Angel Publishing®

DIVINE CIRCUS ORACLE
Guidance for a Life of Sacred Subversion & Creative Confidence

Alana Fairchild
Artwork by various artists

Your spirit thrives in freedom and refuses to be constrained by stereotypes. This brilliantly rebellious part of you claims your authentic path and passionate purpose with gusto, caring not whether there is logic or lunacy at its heart. More than ever, the human collective needs bold-spirited individuals willing to live the loving and joyous wisdom of their hearts.

44 cards + 136-page guidebook packaged in a hardcover box.
ISBN: 978-1-922161-97-0

For more information on this or
any Blue Angel Publishing® release,
please visit our website at:

www.blueangelonline.com